40 Day Devotional Journal

Whole New You

Development is necessary

By: LaToya J

To:

From:

Date:

© 2025 | Latoya J

ISBN: 978-0-578-26426-4

All rights reserved. No portion of this book may be reproduced mechanically, electronically, or by any other means, including photocopying, without written permission of the publisher. It is illegal to copy this book, post it on a website, or distribute it by any other means without permission from the publisher.

Limits of Liability and Disclaimer of Warranty
The author and publisher shall not be liable for your misuse of this material. This book is strictly for informational and educational purposes.

NLT
Scripture taken from the Holy Bible New Living Translation® Copyright © 1996, 2004, 2007, 2013, 2015 by Tyndale House Foundation.

Warning – Disclaimer
The purpose of this book is to educate and entertain. The author and/or publisher do not guarantee that anyone following these techniques, suggestions, tips, ideas, or strategies will become successful. The author and/or publisher shall have neither liability nor responsibility to anyone concerning any loss or damage caused, or alleged to be caused, directly or indirectly by the information contained in this book.

Welcome!

This journal was created for the woman who is weary in the waiting. Learn to embrace God's rhythm, surrender control, trust God's process, and move forward in faith towards purpose. Prioritize yourself without guilt and embrace the development.

Using this journal

SCRIPTURE

The word of God is important to follow when navigating life experiences. Anchor your growth using God's word.

DEVOTIONAL

Relating the scripture to speaking to identity, purpose, and true worth.

JOURNAL PROMPT

Use the Holy Spirit as your guide to answer specific questions

ACTION TIP

Exercise your faith by taking the small, faith-based steps to move toward clarity & confidence in their purpose.

La Toya J

Day 1

Identify Your Routine

Every morning you wake up following the same routine because that's what you've always done. You show up, handle responsibilities, and do what's expected. Yet deep inside, you feel a pull towards something greater. The repetition isn't always the problem; it's the lack of intentionality within it.

David's prayer in Psalm 139 is a bold ask: "Search me, test me, know my heart." He wasn't afraid of what God would uncover. He invited it. That kind of openness allows God to show us where we've disconnected, grown numb, or are simply surviving instead of living.

> Search me, O God, and know my heart; test me and know my anxious thoughts.
> Psalm 139:23

Maybe your daily routine has become too routine. What once gave life now feels draining. Today, ask God to reveal those places. He's not showing you to shame you, but to shift you. That tug in your spirit? That's Him saying, "There's more."

You have a vision for your life but instead of stepping into it, you push it to the side telling yourself "one day." What if "one day" never comes? What if staying in the comfortable, the predictable, the safe is what's keeping you stuck?

It is in recognizing that your gifts are already enough. That you don't have to chase opportunities. You have to walk in obedience. The goal isn't just to work harder but to align yourself with what God has already placed inside of you.

This means step forward boldly. It means refusing to let fear dictate your moves. It means embracing the fact that you were created for more than just getting by. This is your invitation to move from just doing to a life of purpose. No more waiting, no more hesitating. It is time to build the life God has called you to live.

JOURNAL PROMPT

Reflect on your daily routine. What parts of your life feel repetitive and unfulfilling? Where are you simply going through the motions?

―――――――――――――――――――
―――――――――――――――――――
―――――――――――――――――――
―――――――――――――――――――
―――――――――――――――――――
―――――――――――――――――――
―――――――――――――――――――
―――――――――――――――――――
―――――――――――――――――――
―――――――――――――――――――
―――――――――――――――――――

Action tip

Choose one repetitive task today (like commuting, making breakfast, or cleaning), and turn it into a sacred moment. Add prayer, worship, or reflection to that space to reclaim it with intention and presence.

Day 2

Recognize Disconnection

It is very possible to have met all the accomplishments, hit every milestone, reached every goal, and yet feel as if something is off. You have probably ignored it. You told yourself you were just tired and that the next goal would finally bring the fulfillment you were searching for. But deep down you know this isn't just exhaustion. It is a disconnect. Somewhere along the way you lost yourself.

You're doing the work but you don't feel God in it anymore. You're moving and achieving yet you feel empty. You're in the middle of what should be success but instead of feeling accomplished you feel lost. That's because success without purpose is just motion. If God isn't at the center of it all no amount of achievement will ever fill the void.

This is the wake-up call. You weren't created just to reach the next level. You were created for something deeper, more meaningful, more lasting. So now ask yourself are you truly doing what you were called to do, or are you just doing what looks good on paper?

> Remain in me, and I will remain in you. For a branch cannot produce fruit if it is severed from the vine, and you cannot be fruitful unless you remain in me.
> John 15:4

It's time to stop chasing success that leaves you empty and start walking in purpose that fulfills you. It's time to stop striving and start aligning bringing God back to the center of your life, your work, and your decisions.

When you do everything shifts. The work stops feeling heavy. The pressure stops controlling you. The success you build isn't just impressive it's impactful. It carries meaning. It brings peace.

This is your moment to let go of the empty hustle and start living with divine intention. You were made to live fully, deeply, and purposefully.

JOURNAL PROMPT

Where in your life have you been chasing achievement more than purpose? How can you shift your focus to align your work with God's will for you?

_____
_____
_____
_____
_____
_____
_____
_____
_____
_____

Action tip

Start by setting aside intentional time each day for prayer, scripture reading, and quiet reflection, even if it's just 10-15 minutes. During this time, ask God to reveal areas where you've become disconnected from Him, yourself, or others, and seek His guidance on how to restore those connections.

Day 3 — Examine Your Intentions

You are the woman who shows up. You do what is expected. You handle your responsibilities. You pour into others, support them, and work hard to succeed. On paper you're doing everything right. But deep down, you can't help but wonder: "Am I truly walking in my purpose or am I just going through the motions?"

At some point you have to ask yourself: Why do I do what I do? Are you moving from a place of passion or pressure? Are you serving because you love it or because it's expected of you? Are you striving to please God or to prove yourself to people?

It's easy to get caught up in performing for approval, chasing validation instead of purpose. The world applauds achievement but achievement without alignment leaves you empty. You might be meeting expectations but are you truly fulfilled?

This could be why you feel unsettled, even after hitting every milestone because deep inside, you know there's more. More than just showing up. You weren't created to perform. You were created to impact.

> People may be pure in their own eyes, but the Lord examines their motives.
> Proverbs 16:2

It's time to pause and examine your motives. Where is your work coming from? Is it flowing from a place of joy, calling, and passion? Has it become something you do because it's what you've always done? God didn't call you to live a life of obligation. He called you to live a life of purpose.

When you shift from obligation to alignment, everything changes. You no longer feel drained from overextending yourself to meet unrealistic expectations. You feel fueled because you're walking in what God designed for you. This is your invitation to stop striving and start aligning. To uncover those hidden gifts, embrace the calling on your life, and move forward with clarity and confidence. You were made for more and it's time to step into it.

JOURNAL PROMPT

Consider the motivations behind your daily actions. Are you acting out of obligation, fear, or desire for approval? What would change if your intentions were aligned with your true purpose?

_____

_____

_____

_____

_____

_____

_____

_____

_____

_____

_____

_____

Action tip

make a commitment to act from a place of love, service, and alignment with God's will rather than external pressures. Practice asking yourself before each task, "Is this aligned with my purpose and values?" If not, consider adjusting your approach or letting go of that task.

Day | 4

Choosing Purpose Over Perfection

I know for sure you are the woman everyone counts on. With every step, you told yourself this is success. So when the next opportunity came, the bigger role, you didn't stop to question it. You stepped in thinking this was the natural progression. But then something shifted.

What once felt fulfilling became draining. The weight of expectations grew heavier. You told yourself to push through because that's what strong women do, right? They endure. They adapt. They make it work.

> Do not conform to the pattern of this world, but be transformed by the renewing of your mind. — Romans 12:2

Truth is endurance without alignment will exhaust you. At some point you have to ask yourself am I pursuing purpose, or am I just performing? Am I here because I'm called to this or because it looks good on paper? Am I serving from a place of passion or just proving that I can handle it? Am I building a life that fuels me or one that just impresses others?

It's easy to get caught in the cycle of performance but success without purpose will never be enough. It's time to break free. Your gifts were never meant to burden you; they were meant to bless you and bless others.

Choosing purpose over performance requires courage. It means being honest about what drains you and what excites you. It means being willing to let go of what seems like success to step into what actually fulfills you. You don't have to prove yourself. You are already enough. It's time to stop performing for approval and start walking in the life God created for you.

JOURNAL PROMPT

Reflect on the external pressures and expectations that influence your actions. How have these shaped your current routine? What would it look like to let go of these pressures?

_____
_____
_____
_____
_____
_____
_____
_____
_____
_____
_____
_____

Action tip

Take inventory of your current roles and responsibilities. ask yourself these three questions for each: Does this energize me or drain me? Am I doing this out of fear, pride, or the need for approval? Does this align with the gifts, passions, and purpose God has placed within me?

Once you've answered these questions, identify one area in your life where you're operating out of obligation or fear rather than purpose. Take one bold step this week to release it.

Day 5 — Assess Your Priorities

You are exhausted! You keep pushing. You make people proud. You check off every goal. The one thing you can't seem to check off? Fulfillment.

Not everything that looks good is beneficial. Not everything that fills your time fills your soul. The real question isn't "Am I doing enough?" but "Am I doing what God has called me to do?"

> "You say, 'I am allowed to do anything'—but not everything is good for you. You say, 'I am allowed to do anything'—but not everything is beneficial." — 1 Corinthians 10:23

- Are you running on empty because you're chasing productivity instead of purpose?
- Are you saying "yes" to everything but "no" to what truly matters?
- Are you confusing movement with meaning?

God never called you to live a life of constant striving. He called you to live a life of alignment. A life where your priorities match His. A life where you operate from peace, not pressure. It's okay to step back and reassess.

It's okay to ask, "God what's most important in this season?" When you do you'll stop chasing empty achievements and start living with real intention. You'll stop trying to prove yourself and start walking in purpose.

JOURNAL PROMPT

Take a moment to reflect on the areas of your life where you feel stretched too thin. Ask yourself: What are the activities or commitments that drain me the most? Am I doing these things because God has called me to, or because I feel obligated? What is one thing I can step back from to create space for what matters most in this season?
Write down a prayer of surrender, asking God to reveal what is most important for you to focus on right now.

___

Action tip

This week, choose one commitment or activity to evaluate. Pray about whether it aligns with your current season and God's will for you. If it doesn't, take a practical step to release it—delegate, decline, or set boundaries. Then use the time you've reclaimed to focus on intentional growth, prayer, or rest.

Day 6 — Submit and Surrender

You have done the work, sat with your thoughts, traced the patterns, and pinpointed the things that keep you bound. You see it clearly now. The frustration, the cycles, the feeling of being stuck, it's all rooted in what you're still carrying. You know it's time to let go. You don't want to hold on to this weight any longer yet releasing feels just as heavy as keeping it.

Surrender is where true transformation begins. If I will be honest, it's not always pretty. It's not just whispering a polished prayer. Sometimes it's an ugly cry. The kind that leaves you breathless, face buried in your hands, asking God, what now? It's admitting you don't have all the answers, forgiving people who never even apologized, and choosing to trust God's process over your own timeline.

> "Give your burdens to the Lord, and he will take care of you. He will not permit the godly to slip and fall."- Psalm 55:22

Releasing means loosening your grip on what you thought life should look like and allowing God to step in. It's bringing your whole self, every wound, every disappointment, every unanswered question before Him and saying, I don't know how but I trust You will. When you do you make room for God's peace to settle in. The weight lifts. The cycle breaks, and you walk lighter. Not because life is suddenly easy, but because you've given the burden to the only One strong enough to carry it.

Invite God into your healing process (Psalm 147:3). Trust God's process and surrender your fears, dreams, and timeline to Him (Proverbs 3:5-6). Surrender your struggles to God. Reestablish your connection with Him and embrace the peace that comes from trusting His plan.

JOURNAL PROMPT

What are you still holding onto that God is asking you to release? Write a letter to God, expressing what has been weighing on you. Then, imagine what it would feel like to let it go. What changes when you trust God fully in this area?

_____
_____
_____
_____
_____
_____
_____
_____
_____
_____
_____
_____

Action tip

Set aside time today to physically symbolize surrender. Whether it's writing down what you're releasing and tearing it up, praying out loud with honesty, or lifting your hands in worship, make an intentional move toward letting go. Then, each time doubt creeps in, remind yourself: I've already given this to God.

Day 7 — Identity in Christ

Growing up we are taught to define ourselves by the roles we play and the people around us. "Who are you?" is almost always answered by where you're from, your family, your job, or the things you've achieved. While those parts of us might be true, they are not the whole story. Those things shift and change. Jobs end, relationships evolve, achievements fade. If we base our identity solely on these temporary things, we'll constantly find ourselves in an identity crisis reshaping who we are every time life throws us a curveball.

Here's the truth that changes everything. Your identity isn't in what you do or who you know. It's in who God says you are. You were made in His image, designed to reflect His glory, His creativity, and His power. Without understanding this truth it's easy to fall into cycles of fear and insecurity.

When you don't know your true identity you'll find yourself frustrated, questioning your worth, and taking on labels that don't belong to you. You are not the lies you've been told. You are not inadequate, incapable, or insignificant. You are a reflection of God Himself crafted with purpose, value, and authority.

> "So God created human beings in his own image. In the image of God he created them; male and female he created them."
> —Genesis 1:27

The more you know God, the more you'll discover yourself. His Word is the blueprint for your identity. He says you're fearfully and wonderfully made. A masterpiece created for good works. When you embrace who He says you are fear loses its grip, insecurities begin to fade, and you'll start walking in the authority that's been yours all along.

If you want to truly know who you are, you have to study the One who made you. Dig deep into His Word, spend time in His presence, and let Him reveal to you the beauty and power He's placed inside of you. Knowing Him is the key to knowing yourself.

JOURNAL PROMPT

Reflect on the labels you've worn throughout your life. Which ones came from others, and which ones did you place on yourself? How do these labels compare to what God says about you?

_____
_____
_____
_____
_____
_____
_____
_____
_____
_____
_____
_____

Action tip

Write down three truths from Scripture about your identity in Christ. How can you begin to live as though these truths are your reality?

Day. | 8
Developed in the tough dry place

The dry tough place. It is a space that feels lonely, quiet, and sometimes unsettling. It's the place where you start questioning everything. "God, are You here? Do You see me? The journey through this place is tough, but it's also nurturing. It's here that God tests, develops, and affirms you, just as He did with His Son, Jesus.

Even Jesus wasn't exempt from this process. Before He stepped into His public ministry, the Spirit led Him into the wilderness for 40 days. This tough place wasn't meant to destroy Him but to strengthen Him for what was to come.

Realize that this space and place is where God is preparing us for our future selves. It's where He prunes us, builds our faith muscles, and shapes our character to handle the promises He's spoken over us.

> Then Jesus told him, "Go back home. Your son will live!" And the man believed what Jesus said and started home. While the man was on his way, some of his servants met him with the news that his son was alive and well.
> John 4:50-51

This journey of development often looks like clinging to God's word. It's a place of going back to God over and over, seeking direction, clarity, and reassurance. Think about the official in John 4. He had to take Jesus at His word when He said, "Your son will live." There was no evidence, no immediate confirmation. Just the word. And with that word, he walked the journey back home alone, trusting God during a tough time. I imagine every step of that walk deepened his faith and built his trust.

That is the purpose of this place. Not to isolate you but to develop you. To mature you. To teach you to trust God even when you don't see the end from the beginning. He's calling you closer. The question is: Do you trust Him enough to stay?

JOURNAL PROMPT

Write about a promise or word from God that you're holding on to right now. What steps can you take to trust Him more deeply while you wait?

_____
_____
_____
_____
_____
_____
_____
_____
_____
_____
_____
_____

Action tip

Identify one area of your life where you're struggling to trust God. Write down the specific promise or scripture that speaks to this situation. For the next week, dedicate 5-10 minutes each day to meditate on that promise, pray over it, and take one small faith-based action aligned with trusting God.

Day 9 — The Wilderness: Your Training Ground

There is a moment in every woman's journey where she finds herself in a season that feels barren. It's the in-between place. The space after the promise is spoken but before it is fulfilled. Maybe you feel it now. Like you're stuck, unseen, and exhausted from the waiting. You've been obedient, you've trusted God, and yet you find yourself wandering, wondering, "What is happening?"

Jesus knew this place well. Before His ministry began, He was led into the wilderness. Not by accident, not by consequence, but by the Spirit of God and if the Son of God had to go through a season of testing and refinement before stepping fully into His purpose, so will we.

> "Remember how the Lord your God led you through the wilderness for these forty years, humbling you and testing you to prove your character, and to find out whether or not you would obey his commands."
> – Deuteronomy 8:2

Here is the truth no one tells you. The wilderness is not a punishment. It is preparation. This is the season where God matures you, strengthens your faith, and equips you for the weight of the promise. The wilderness reveals your heart. What's really in you when no one is watching, when things aren't going your way, when the dream feels delayed. Will you trust God or will you give up?

This place is not meant to break you but to build you. Your endurance, your wisdom, your dependence on God, all of it is built here. But how do you survive the wilderness without losing yourself? Remember God's promises. His Word does not return void. What He spoke over you will come to pass. Strengthen yourself spiritually and physically. The enemy will try to weaken you but staying in God's presence keeps you fortified. Walk in wisdom and discernment. Every opportunity is not from God. Stay sharp. Keep moving forward. Now is not the time to give up. What's ahead is greater than what's behind.

The wilderness can feel like a season of wandering, wanting, and waiting but it is also the place where you become completely dependent on God. Trust that He is leading you through this and on the other side, you'll be stronger, wiser, and fully prepared for what He has called you to do.

JOURNAL PROMPT

What is God revealing about you in this season? Are there areas of your heart that He is refining? Write about how you can shift your perspective to see this as preparation rather than punishment.

_____
_____
_____
_____
_____
_____
_____
_____
_____
_____
_____

Action tip

Create a "Wilderness Survival Kit" by writing down three scriptures that remind you of God's promises. Keep them in a place where you can read them daily. Declare them over your life when doubt tries to creep in. Include songs, prayer points and share with your close circle for accountability

You are not lost. You are in training. And when you come out of this, you will be ready for everything God has for you.

Day 10 — Life with the Holy Spirit

Having the Holy Spirit is key to doing this journey. It's like having your own personal counselor and guide within you. You may be able to navigate some on your own but eventually, you will be exhausted, frustrated, and lost. Jesus promised you the gift of the Holy Spirit; as it is something you have all time access to.

Jesus came to earth, stepped forward into time, faced temptations, challenges, and hardship, just as today, with only one tool, His relationship with the Holy Spirit. That same Spirit is available to you. Right now. Always.

The Holy Spirit is your personal guide. When you don't know what to do, he gives wisdom and strategy. When you're about to make the wrong turn, he gets you back in alignment. He gives discernment when something isn't right.

> "But you will receive power when the Holy Spirit comes upon you. And you will be my witnesses, telling people about me everywhere—in Jerusalem, throughout Judea, in Samaria, and to the ends of the earth." – Acts 1:8

Some of the greatest decisions you'll ever make will not come from logic, but from the Holy Spirit. The reason why so many women feel lost, exhausted, and disconnected isnt because they arent capable. It's because they are trying to do God's work without God's power. To sum this all up, you cannot fully walk in your purpose without Him. Jesus gave us power to demonstrate the same works He did, and even greater works.

Before the disciples were to leave Jerusalem, they had to receive the promise of the Holy Spirit (Acts 1:4). Without the power of the Holy Spirit, they would not have the capacity, wisdom, and authority needed to carry out their assignment. The same is true for you. You were created for greater works but the greater works requires greater power. That power doesn't come from gifts or experience but from an intimate relationship with the Holy Spirit. With the Holy Spirit guiding you, there is no limit to what God can do through you.

JOURNAL PROMPT

In what areas of your life have you been relying on your own strength instead of the Holy Spirit? How can you invite the Holy Spirit to guide you more intentionally?

―――――――――――――――――――――
―――――――――――――――――――――
―――――――――――――――――――――
―――――――――――――――――――――
―――――――――――――――――――――
―――――――――――――――――――――
―――――――――――――――――――――
―――――――――――――――――――――
―――――――――――――――――――――
―――――――――――――――――――――
―――――――――――――――――――――
―――――――――――――――――――――
―――――――――――――――――――――
―――――――――――――――――――――

Action tip

Each morning this week, pause before making any major decisions (big or small) and ask the Holy Spirit for wisdom. Write down any insights, feelings, or nudges you receive and reflect on how they align with God's direction.

Day 11

Fear has to go

What is the number one thing that keeps us from stepping fully into our purpose? Fear. Fear of not being good enough. Fear of not knowing where to start. Fear of the unknown.

It creeps in whispering doubts and making us hesitate. We shrink back instead of stepping forward. We second-guess every move, overthink every decision, and before we know it, we've convinced ourselves that we're not capable, not ready, not worthy.

Fear is a self-fulfilling prophecy. Just like Job said, "What I always feared has happened to me. What I dreaded has come true." (Job 3:25)

When we give fear a seat at the table, it starts calling the shots. It keeps us stuck in cycles of hesitation and smallness, robbing us of the fullness God has for us. The truth is fear is not of God.

> "For God has not given us a spirit of fear and timidity, but of power, love, and self-discipline."
> – 2 Timothy 1:7

"For God has not given us a spirit of fear and timidity, but of power, love, and self-discipline." (2 Timothy 1:7, NLT)

God never intended for us to live in fear. He is the creator of solutions, the giver of wisdom, and the one who speaks things into existence. When uncertainty rises up, fear doesn't have to be the automatic response. Instead, we can anchor ourselves in His love, His power, and His peace.

It's time to stop making decisions from fear and start moving in faith. God-sized dreams require God-filled confidence. When we replace fear with faith, we step into the boldness of who we were created to be.

Today, choose courage. Break free. Step forward and trust that what God has for you is already written in His perfect plan.

JOURNAL PROMPT

Where in your life is fear keeping you from moving forward? What would it look like to replace that fear with faith?

_____
_____
_____
_____
_____
_____
_____
_____
_____
_____
_____
_____
_____

Action tip

Identify one fear that has been holding you back. Write it down, then next to it, write a truth from God's Word that replaces that fear. Speak that truth over yourself daily and take one bold step toward what you've been avoiding.

Day 12 — Letting Go of the Old

We like to think that because we've always been a certain way that that is just who we are. That our upbringing, our past experiences, and the beliefs we inherited have solidified our identity. But what if they've only shaped a version of you that God never intended for you to stay in?

To embrace what's coming, you have to release what was. Old mindsets, toxic cycles, expired relationships. They may have once served a purpose, but they can't go where you're headed. You can't step into new while still clinging to the old.

Have you ever stopped and realized that you've been living according to the world's standards instead of your true calling? That for years, you operated from a place of rejection, dysfunction, or fear without even realizing it? But now something inside of you is shifting. You're waking up. You're being transformed. You're renewing your mind daily. That is the thing about transformation. It requires release.

> This means that anyone who belongs to Christ has become a new person. The old life is gone; a new life has begun!" – 2 Corinthians 5:17

Being whole means letting go of the habits, beliefs, and survival tactics you picked up just to make it through. It means changing your mindset and choosing to walk in freedom. It means no longer holding yourself hostage to what was but boldly stepping into who you were always meant to be.

Because it's more than just bearing fruit. Your roots have to be healthy. Dead roots can't produce life. If you're still attached to what no longer serves you, how can you expect to flourish?

Shedding the old isn't easy. It will stretch you. It will challenge everything you thought you knew. But on the other side of that work is freedom, clarity, authenticity, and purpose. Do the work. You owe it to yourself.

JOURNAL PROMPT

What old mindsets, habits, or beliefs have you been holding onto that no longer serve your growth? What would it look like to fully release them and embrace the new?

_____
_____
_____
_____
_____
_____
_____
_____
_____
_____
_____
_____

Action tip

Identify one belief or habit from your past that you know is keeping you from stepping into your purpose. Write it down, then replace it with truth. Speak it over yourself daily and start walking in it.

Day 13

Trusting Gods timing

There are moments in life when we need God to act fast. When the pressure is mounting, and the weight of waiting feels unbearable. We pray, we plead, we cry out for Him to move now. But if there's one thing I've learned, it's this: God does not operate on our timeline. He is the Author and Finisher of our faith. He knows the right time to release blessings, open doors, and shift circumstances. No amount of urgency, frustration, or emotion moves Him out of His divine timing.

The story of Lazarus is the perfect example. In John 11, Martha stood before Jesus, grief stricken and frustrated. "Lord, if you had been here, my brother would not have died." She believed Jesus could heal, but she struggled with His timing. She didn't yet see that God's delay was not His denial. What she thought was too late was actually setting the stage for something greater than she imagined, the resurrection of her brother.

> "for there is a time and a way for everything, even when a person is in trouble."- Ecclesiastes 8:6

Isn't that just like us that when we feel delayed, we assume God isn't listening. We take matters into our own hands, forcing our way through doors He never opened. Or we get angry and withdraw from Him completely. Here's the truth: what hasn't happened yet, isn't necessary for today.

That is why Jesus teaches us to pray, "Give us this day our daily bread." (Matthew 6:11, NLT). It's a reminder that whatever you truly need, God will provide for today. If it hasn't come yet, it's either not a necessity, or not time. No matter how much we think we're ready, God won't release something prematurely. He isn't just concerned about giving us what we want. He's committed to our growth, maturity, and preparation for the next level. If you're waiting, trust this: God is not withholding from you. He is preparing you. His timing is perfect, and when He moves, it will be right on time.

JOURNAL PROMPT

Where in your life are you struggling with God's timing? How can you shift your perspective from frustration to trust, believing that His delays are for your good?

_____
_____
_____
_____
_____
_____
_____
_____
_____
_____
_____
_____

Action tip

Identify one area where you've been trying to force a breakthrough instead of waiting on God. Write a surrender statement, releasing it back to Him in faith. Let today be a step toward trusting His perfect timing.

Day 14 — Grieve but Move

There comes a time when God calls you to move suddenly, swiftly, and without apology. It's an urgent request, a divine push that forces you to leave behind what you once knew.

To be honest change is scary. It's one thing to pray for growth, but when God starts pulling you into new territory, new levels, and new assignments, that's when the reality sets in.

Elevation requires separation. Old mindsets, familiar habits, and even long standing relationships may not fit where God is taking you and that's hard. You may find yourself grieving the life you once had but remember that you can grieve and grow at the same time.

> "But forget all that— it is nothing compared to what I am going to do. For I am about to do something new. See, I have already begun! Do you not see it?" – Isaiah 43:18-19

It's okay to feel the loss. It's okay to miss what was while stepping into what is. Let yourself process the emotions, but don't let them keep you stuck. The worst thing you can do is pause for too long in a place God has called you to leave.

You are no longer an average person. You are elevating. You are being called higher. You are stepping into something greater, something that requires a stronger, more disciplined, more refined version of you. Yes, that means letting go of connections that no longer align. You may grieve pulling away from friends and from environments that no longer serve you but necessary endings make space for divine beginnings.

God sees your obedience, your willingness to move even when it hurts and in the middle of it all, He is whispering: "I'm proud of you." Honor your emotions, but keep walking forward. Feel your feelings, but don't lose momentum. A new version of you is emerging and she's worth everything you had to leave behind.

JOURNAL PROMPT

What are you currently grieving as you move forward? How can you honor your feelings while staying committed to the new season God is leading you into?

_____
_____
_____
_____
_____
_____
_____
_____
_____
_____
_____
_____

Action tip

Write a "letting go" letter to what (or who) you're releasing. Acknowledge what it meant to you, express gratitude for what it taught you, and declare your readiness to step into what's next. Then, read it aloud and surrender it to God. You are moving forward.

Day 15 — Spiritual warfare

The moment you decide to walk boldly in your calling and the moment you receive a word that confirms your next level, Heaven rejoices, but so does hell. Not in celebration, but in opposition.

The enemy sees what's coming. He knows that if you actually step into what God has for you chains will break, lives will change, and the Kingdom will advance. So what does he do? Steals your joy, peace, and focus. He kills your dreams, goals, and passion. He destroys your progression and future.

For many of us this works. We get discouraged. We get distracted. We start looking at our problems instead of the promise.

> "We are human, but we don't wage war as humans do. We use God's mighty weapons, not worldly weapons, to knock down the strongholds of human reasoning and to destroy false arguments." – 2 Corinthians 10:3-4

What's the problem? Too many believers are trying to fight spiritual battles with worldly weapons. You cannot defeat a spiritual enemy with carnal strategies. The reason so many feel stuck, overwhelmed, or constantly under attack is because they're fighting in their own strength instead of God's power. You need the right weapons.

Worship, Prayer, Fasting, Obedience, Serving, Communion, The Armor of God, Declaring His Word, Renewing Your Mind. This is how you fight. Not by shrinking back. Not by going silent. You do it by standing firm, knowing you already have the victory in Christ. The enemy doesn't fear those who go through the motions. He fears those who know their authority.

So, suit up. Trust God's strategy. Take your thoughts captive and move forward knowing that this battle is already won. The abundant life God promised is still yours if you're willing to fight for it.

JOURNAL PROMPT

Where in your life have you been trying to fight battles in your own strength? How can you start using spiritual weapons instead?

_____
_____
_____
_____
_____
_____
_____
_____
_____
_____
_____
_____

Action tip

Choose one spiritual weapon from the list (prayer, worship, fasting, declaring scripture, etc.) and commit to using it intentionally for the next seven days. Write down the shifts you notice—spiritually, mentally, and emotionally.

Day 16 — Sovereign in Suffering

Becoming like Christ. That's the goal right? To reflect His love, His wisdom, His power. What happens when following Him doesn't look like walking on water, multiplying loaves, or healing the sick? What happens when it looks like waiting, loss, rejection, or walking a road you never would have chosen for yourself? Nobody really talks about that part.

Jesus didn't just live in glory. He suffered and He told us we would too (John 16:33). Yet, when suffering shows up in our own lives, we often ask, God, where are You? Did I do something wrong? Have You forgotten me? Suffering is not proof of God's absence. It's proof that we're sharing in His story.

God never wastes pain. In suffering, we see sides of Him we might not have otherwise known Comforter, Strength, Healer, Peace. In suffering our faith is stretched. Our character is refined. Our endurance is built. While it may not feel like it in the moment, we're becoming stronger, wiser, and more like Him.

> "We can rejoice, too, when we run into problems and trials, for we know that they help us develop endurance. And endurance develops strength of character, and character strengthens our confident hope of salvation."- Romans 5:3-4

Paul reminds us that suffering produces endurance and endurance strengthens our character. This means the struggle isn't just something to survive. It's something God is using to transform us. This season isn't the end of your story. It's a chapter leading to glory.

Do not let suffering make you doubt God's love for you. Instead, let it drive you deeper into Him. Read His Word. Remind Him, and yourself of His promises. Keep your faith on display, and trust that if you're sharing in His sufferings now, you will also share in His glory.

JOURNAL PROMPT

Think about a difficult season in your life. How did it shape you? In what ways did you experience God differently? Write about how God can use your current struggles for your growth and transformation.

_____
_____
_____
_____
_____
_____
_____
_____
_____
_____
_____
_____

Action tip

Instead of asking Why is this happening? shift your perspective and ask What is God teaching me through this? This week, write down one lesson God is revealing to you in your current season. Find a scripture that speaks to it, and meditate on it daily.

Day 17 — The Power of Rest

The world glorifies the grind. We hear it everywhere. "No sleep. No days off. Hustle harder." It's as if our worth is measured by exhaustion, as if proving ourselves means pushing past every limit. Society teaches us that if we stop, we'll fall behind. But what if I told you that real success isn't found in running yourself into the ground? That rest is not a weakness. It's a strategy.

Even Jesus, who carried the weight of the world, made rest a priority. After pouring out, healing, and teaching, He turned to His disciples and said, "Come with me by yourselves to a quiet place and get some rest." (Mark 6:31, NLT). He understood something we often forget: You cannot pour from an empty cup. You cannot receive fresh vision with a clouded mind. You cannot lead effectively when you're running on fumes.

> "Then Jesus said, 'Let's go off by ourselves to a quiet place and rest awhile.' He said this because there were so many people coming and going that Jesus and his apostles didn't even have time to eat." – Mark 6:31

Yet, how often do we ignore the warning signs? The burnout, the frustration, the exhaustion we convince ourselves is "normal"? Many of us aren't just tired, we are spiritually, mentally, and emotionally depleted. We've been running in survival mode for so long that we don't even recognize what true restoration feels like. Remember God provides even in rest.

There are seven types of rest—physical, mental, emotional, sensory, creative, social, and spiritual. Each one is necessary. Your next level, your next breakthrough, your next divine opportunity; it requires energy, focus, and endurance. You cannot step into what God has for you if you're too drained to receive it.

Stop wearing burnout as a badge of honor. Rest is a power move. It's how you sustain the call on your life. It's how you move from striving to thriving. It's how you hear God clearly, build strength, and operate in divine alignment. Because at the end of the day, true success doesn't come from our frantic effort. It comes from unwavering faith and trust in God's provision. Rest is not a delay. It's a setup for what's next.

JOURNAL PROMPT

In what areas of your life have you been running on empty? How can you begin to prioritize rest as a form of obedience and trust in God's provision?

_____
_____
_____
_____
_____
_____
_____
_____
_____
_____
_____
_____

Action tip

Identify one type of rest you've been neglecting (physical, mental, emotional, sensory, creative, social, or spiritual). This week, schedule intentional time to pause and refill in that area. Make room for rest as a strategy, not an afterthought.

Day 18 — Cost of Comparison

I used to say it all the time half joking, half wishing: If I had that voice, I'd never stop singing. It seemed harmless. Just an offhand comment. But one day, God checked me. Why do you think you need that voice?

The question hit differently because the truth was deep down I wasn't just admiring someone else's gift. I was questioning my own. I saw their talent, platform, and influence, and something in me whispered, If I had that, maybe I'd be more valuable. Maybe I'd be seen.

> "Pay careful attention to your own work, for then you will get the satisfaction of a job well done, and you won't need to compare yourself to anyone else." - Galatians 6:4

Comparison is subtle like that. It doesn't always show up as jealousy. Sometimes it looks like innocent admiration that slowly turns into silent discontent. It makes you see your life through the lens of lack instead of purpose. It convinces you that what God gave you isn't enough. That He must have been more intentional when He made the person you are admiring.

The truth is God does not make mistakes. You weren't meant to have their calling. You were designed with your specific gifts, personality, and story for a reason. The moment you start wishing for someone else's, you start rejecting your own.

Comparison distorts your identity. It tells you that who you are is not enough. But God says otherwise. He says I placed you exactly where I wanted you. I put gifts inside of you that this world needs. I don't need another version of her. I need YOU.

What if we stopped looking to the left and right, measuring our worth against someone else's highlight reel? What if we actually embraced who we are as we are, believing that God's design is intentional? That's where freedom is. That's where purpose starts. Fulfillment doesn't come from being more like the next person. It comes from being fully you.

JOURNAL PROMPT

Where in your life have you fallen into comparison? How has it shaped the way you see yourself? Write about a time when you felt like what you had wasn't enough. Now, ask God to shift your perspective—to help you see yourself the way He sees you.

_____
_____
_____
_____
_____
_____
_____
_____
_____
_____
_____
_____
_____

Action tip

Every time you catch yourself comparing, stop and replace the thought with truth. Write down one thing that makes you uniquely you—a gift, a personality trait, a strength—and thank God for it. Practice shifting your focus from what you lack to what God has already placed inside you.

Day 19 — Character Refinement

Character is not built in a single moment. It's formed in the quiet spaces when no one is watching, when decisions seem small, and when daily habits slowly shape who we become.

Truth is, who you spend the most time with influences who you become. If you spend time with God leaning into His word, aligning your heart with His, and allowing Him to lead, you will start to reflect His nature in ways you never imagined. But this journey isn't just about knowing God; it's about becoming like Him.

Discipleship is a call to mirror Christ in our decisions, our interactions, and even in the way we handle failure. It's about shifting our desires to align with His, letting what breaks His heart break ours, and walking with a spirit of love, integrity, and purpose.

> "And endurance develops strength of character, and character strengthens our confident hope of salvation." – Romans 5:4

The fruits of the Spirit love, joy, peace, patience, kindness, goodness, faithfulness, gentleness, and self-control aren't just nice virtues. They are markers of a transformed life, proof that we are becoming who we were created to be. Mistakes will happen. The goal isn't perfection, it's progress.

God isn't looking for flawlessness. He's looking for faithfulness. He wants to know that He can trust you with the promises He has for your life. The tests and trials you face aren't to break you but to build you, refinie your character, strengthen your endurance, and prepare you for greater responsibility.

You hold the ability to shape the woman you are becoming. Will you steward the work of your hands and the condition of your heart well? Let God mold you. Let Him prepare you. When the tests come, stand firm knowing that the fire isn't meant to consume you but to refine you because when your character is ready, so is your calling.

JOURNAL PROMPT

What areas of your character are being tested right now? How can you invite God into the process instead of resisting the refinement?

_____
_____
_____
_____
_____
_____
_____
_____
_____
_____
_____
_____

Action tip

Identify one fruit of the Spirit that you struggle with the most (patience, self-control, kindness, etc.). This week, be intentional about practicing it in your daily life. Pray for God's help, take small steps, and reflect on the growth He is producing in you.

Day 20 — Walking in Kingdom Authority

For so long you've been waiting for permission, for validation, for someone to tell you that you are worthy of more. You've spent years following the rules and doing what's expected, Yet deep inside you feel unfulfilled like you're living beneath your potential. Like you were made for more. The truth is you were.

You were never meant to live small. You were never meant to shrink back in fear, second guess your purpose, or wait for someone to hand you the life you were called to walk in. The Kingdom of God is within you. The moment you submitted your life to Christ, you gained access to power, authority, and divine access to Heaven's resources.

> "You won't be able to say, 'Here it is!' or 'It's over there!' For the Kingdom of God is already among you." – Luke 17:21

At the cross Jesus didn't just die for your salvation. He died to give you the keys to the Kingdom. Keys represent access, authority, and ownership. You don't have to beg for what's already yours. However, the enemy's strategy is to convince you that you are powerless, unworthy, and stuck.

It's time to wake up to know who you are in Christ. To stop living as though you are defeated when the same power that raised Jesus from the dead lives inside you.

The authority you walk in comes from your relationship with God. Jesus showed us that His power flowed directly from His intimacy with the Father. The more connected you are to God, the more you operate in your rightful authority.

Once you recognize your Kingdom authority you stop settling. You start praying with boldness, moving with confidence, and making decisions that align with your divine calling. You step into rooms knowing you belong there. You let go of fear because you understand that nothing can take away what God has already given you. When you fully embrace your authority you start building, leading, impacting, and shifting atmospheres. Not by your own strength but through the power of God working within you. The world doesn't change when we wait. It changes when we rise. Let go of fear. Stop waiting for permission. Walk boldly in the authority God has already given you. The Kingdom is within you and it's time to live like it.

JOURNAL PROMPT

Where in your life have you been waiting for permission to walk in the authority God has already given you? What fears or doubts have been holding you back from fully stepping into your purpose?

_____
_____
_____
_____
_____
_____
_____
_____
_____
_____
_____
_____
_____
_____

Action tip

Write down one area of your life where you've been playing small. Now, declare the truth over it. Find a scripture that aligns with God's promises and begin speaking it over yourself daily. Step into your Kingdom authority—starting today.

Day 21 — The Power of Consistency

We love results. We love seeing progress, movement, and signs that our hard work is paying off. But what happens when the results don't come as fast as we expected? Do we stop? Do we slow down? Do we question if we even heard God correctly?

This is where consistency comes in. God doesn't just reward efforts, He rewards faithfulness. He blesses those who keep showing up, even when they don't feel like it. Those who stay committed when no one is clapping. Those who obey even when they don't see immediate change.

> "If you are faithful in little things, you will be faithful in large ones." – Luke 16:10

Consistency is more than a habit. It's evidence of trust. When you keep moving forward, no matter what, you're telling God:
- "I trust You enough to keep going, even when I don't see the full picture."
- "I believe in Your promises, even when they feel far away."
- "I will be faithful, because I know You are faithful."

God honors consistency because it proves that you are a someone He can trust with His assignments. If He can trust you in the small, He can trust you with the big.

Think about it: Would you invest more into someone who only shows up when they feel like it? No. You invest in those who are faithful. That's how God works too. Your consistency in prayer, in showing up for your purpose, in stewarding what He's given you, that is where transformation happens.

Speed isn't a measure of success. Faithfulness is. Even if progress seems slow, even if it feels repetitive, keep going. Keep doing what He asked. Keep showing up, day after day, knowing that every step you take in faith is leading you to the fulfillment of His promises. When you remain consistent, God knows He can trust you and when God trusts you, He releases the next level.

JOURNAL PROMPT

Where in your life have you been inconsistent? What would it look like to commit fully and trust God with the outcome?

_____
_____
_____
_____
_____
_____
_____
_____
_____
_____
_____

Action tip

Choose one area where you've struggled with consistency—prayer, purpose, personal growth, discipline—and commit to it for the next seven days. Write down how it feels to stay the course and trust God with the process.

Day 22 — Serving is Purpose

We live in a world that constantly whispers, "Get yours first." Success is often measured by how much we can accumulate. More money, more status, more recognition. But in the Kingdom of God, the path to purpose isn't about taking. It's about giving.

Serving others isn't just a good deed. It's a lifestyle. It's a reflection of God's love in action, a tangible way to show the compassion we've received. Jesus Himself came not to be served, but to serve. If our Savior saw greatness in humility, why do we struggle to do the same?

True service doesn't seek applause. It's not about doing for those who can return the favor or about being seen. It's about obedience, gratitude, and love. When we fully grasp the depth of what Christ did for us on the cross, we don't serve to gain favor or prove our worth. We serve because we are already loved.

> "For even the Son of Man came not to be served but to serve others and to give his life as a ransom for many." – Mark 10:45

There is freedom in knowing that your value isn't tied to what you do, but in who you are in Him. And yet, God still calls us to serve. Not because He needs us to, but because He knows that serving aligns us with His heart, refines our character, and unlocks deeper purpose.

Don't get so wrapped up in your own journey that you miss the people God has placed around you. Ask Him to position you where He needs you to be a blessing, a light, a vessel. The higher you rise, the greater your responsibility to lift others. True leadership isn't about status. It's about servanthood. Give. Love. Overdeliver and watch how God turns your willingness into a life overflowing with meaning.

JOURNAL PROMPT

Where in your life have you been waiting to be served instead of stepping up to serve? How can you shift your mindset to embrace service as a part of your purpose?

_____
_____
_____
_____
_____
_____
_____
_____
_____
_____
_____
_____
_____
_____

Action tip

This week, find one way to serve someone without expecting anything in return. It could be a small act of kindness, a helping hand, or offering encouragement. Pray for God to open your eyes to opportunities to serve, then act on it.

Day 23 — Peace while Waiting

Waiting on God can feel like you're wasting time with no end in sight. You know He's faithful. You know He has a plan but when the answers don't come quickly, when life feels stuck in a cycle of delays and disappointments, it's easy to get anxious.

The enemy knows this. He preys on our waiting seasons, whispering lies that stir fear, frustration, and insecurity. He wants you to believe that God has forgotten you. That what you're praying for will never happen. That you should take matters into your own hands. Remember this. God's timing is perfect.

"The Lord isn't really being slow about his promise, as some people think. No, he is being patient for your sake." – 2 Peter 3:9 (NLT) Just because you don't see movement doesn't mean God isn't working. Just because the door hasn't opened yet doesn't mean it's locked. Delay is not denial. God is moving behind the scenes, orchestrating things in ways you can't imagine. Your job in the waiting? Keep your peace.

> "Don't worry about anything; instead, pray about everything. Tell God what you need, and thank him for all he has done. Then you will experience God's peace, which exceeds anything we can understand." – Philippians 4:6-7

Do not be anxious. Anxiety rushes what God is still preparing. Rest in the fact that He is never late. The enemy wants you to panic, to doubt, to lose faith. Stand firm, knowing that what God has spoken will come to pass. Do not let emotions dictate your belief. Feel what you need to feel, but do not let those feelings convince you that God is not in control. His track record is flawless. Perfect peace is your portion.

"You will keep in perfect peace all who trust in you, all whose thoughts are fixed on you!" – Isaiah 26:3 (NLT). This means peace isn't found in circumstances. It's found in trust. The more you fix your thoughts on God, the more you train your heart to rest in His sovereignty rather than stress over His timing.

The enemy wants to see you frustrated, questioning, giving up. But you will not break. Instead, you will wait well. You will hold your peace. You will trust that at just the right time, God will do exactly what He promised.

JOURNAL PROMPT

What fears or anxieties have you been carrying in your waiting season? How can you surrender them to God and rest in His peace?

_____
_____
_____
_____
_____
_____
_____
_____
_____
_____
_____
_____

Action tip

Each time worry or fear tries to take over, pause and replace it with gratitude. Instead of stressing over what hasn't happened, thank God for what He's already done. Speak His promises over your situation and choose to wait in peace, not panic.

Day. 24
You Weren't Meant to Do Life Alone

For too long, we've been told that independence is the goal. That needing people is a weakness. That we have to be strong, handle everything on our own, and prove we can carry the weight of life without breaking. But that was never God's design. God works through people. His love, His provision, His comfort it often comes wrapped in the presence of others. We pray for blessings and He answers through a conversation, a helping hand, a shoulder to lean on. When we refuse to embrace community, we block the very thing we're asking for.

When life shifts and you're in transition, pivoting toward purpose, or wrestling with uncertainty you need people who will stand in the gap with you. People who will celebrate your wins, correct you in love, pray with you when you can't find the words, and remind you of who you are when you forget. Romans 12:15 (NLT) says, "Be happy with those who are happy, and weep with those who weep." That's what real community looks like.

> "Be happy with those who are happy, and weep with those who weep." – Romans 12:15

Many of us have convinced ourselves we don't need it. Maybe because we've been hurt before. Maybe because we fear being vulnerable or maybe because we've worn isolation like armor, thinking it's safer than opening up. Growth doesn't happen in isolation. It happens in connection.

Community provides accountability when you start to drift, encouragement when you're weary, fresh perspective when you feel stuck, and space to pour into others just as you are poured into. You don't just receive in the right community you contribute. You help others rise as you rise. That's how God designed it.

So if you've been walking alone, it's time to change that. Your next level isn't meant to be reached in solitude. The support you're afraid to receive is the very thing that will help you step into all that God has for you.

JOURNAL PROMPT

What fears or past experiences have kept you from fully embracing community? What kind of support do you need in this season, and how can you begin to seek out godly connections?

_____
_____
_____
_____
_____
_____
_____
_____
_____
_____
_____
_____
_____

Action tip

Identify one person or group you trust and intentionally engage with them this week. Whether it's opening up about what you're going through, asking for wisdom, or simply spending time together—take one step toward building the community God wants for you.

Day 25 — Fight to Focus

You ever catch yourself scrolling for "just a minute" and suddenly an hour has passed? Watching other people live their lives while your own dreams sit untouched? Distractions don't always look like problems. Sometimes, they look like entertainment, busyness, or even relationships that pull you in every direction except the one God is calling you to.

The enemy is strategic. He knows that if he can keep you occupied with things that drain your energy and waste your time, you'll never have the capacity to step into your calling. Distraction is the enemy's way of keeping you from your destiny.

> "I am saying this for your benefit, not to place restrictions on you. I want you to do whatever will help you serve the Lord best, with as few distractions as possible." - 1 Corithians 7:35

It's not just about social media, endless emails, or constant noise. It's about keeping you too preoccupied to build what God has placed inside of you. Every time you sit down to work on your purpose, something else demands your attention. Before you know it another day has passed, another year has gone by, and you're still saying, "One day, I'll get serious about this."

Think about it. The enemy wouldn't fight so hard to keep you from something that doesn't matter. Your focus, your gifts, your vision, they're a threat. That's why every time you try to move forward there's another delay, another detour, another distraction. Some distractions have names. Some have faces. Some are just mindless routines that steal the hours meant for your calling.

Today, choose to fight back. Eliminate distractions. Set boundaries. Stop consuming and start creating. Stop waiting for the "perfect time" and start making time. Your future is at stake. Your legacy is at stake and God is waiting for you to stop watching and start building.

JOURNAL PROMPT

What distractions have been keeping you from walking fully in your purpose? What steps can you take to remove or reduce them starting today?

_____
_____
_____
_____
_____
_____
_____
_____
_____
_____
_____

Action tip

Set a one-hour distraction-free zone every day this week. Turn off social media notifications, silence unnecessary noise, and dedicate that time solely to what God has called you to do—whether it's praying, planning, creating, or taking action toward your purpose.

Day 26

Time is Currency

Time is one of the most valuable resources God has given us. Unlike money, we can't earn more of it. Unlike possessions, we can't replace it. Once it's spent it's gone. Yet, too often, we find ourselves scattered, overbooked, and exhausted because we haven't mastered the discipline of managing our time well. God is not going to release more into your hands when you are already stretched too thin.

God honors stewardship. If you can't manage what you currently have like your schedule, responsibilities, and commitments, why would He give you more? Success isn't just about doing more. It's about managing well what's already in front of you.

> "Make the most of every opportunity in these evil days."
> – Ephesians 5:16

Did you know that God designed our brains to need rest after 90 minutes of focused work? Science confirms what God already knew. We are not machines. We were created to work in cycles of focus and renewal, not constant grind.

That means true productivity isn't about doing the most. It's about doing the right things at the right time. Wise women plan ahead. Take ownership of your time and set priorities. Disciplined women know when to say no. You must discern what is essential and what can wait. Faithful women follow through. Your commitments matter. Not just to you, but to the people who trust your word. Following through on what you start strengthens your testimony. Through it all, never compromise your time with the Father.

Jesus had a full time ministry, crowds pulling at Him, people demanding His presence, yet He still withdrew to pray. He knew that being busy is not the same as being effective. He surrendered His plans daily, making space to hear from God before making moves. The same applies to you.

Time is a form of currency. Spend it wisely. Manage your responsibilities well, but leave space for God to move. Plan your time well, but remain open to His redirection. Prioritize what truly matters and you'll find that success follows alignment.

JOURNAL PROMPT

Where have you been mismanaging your time? What shifts can you make to ensure that your schedule aligns with God's will and your true priorities?

_____
_____
_____
_____
_____
_____
_____
_____
_____
_____
_____
_____

Action tip

Take a time audit this week. Track where your time is going—work, social media, distractions, family, rest. Then, identify one area where you need better boundaries or adjustments. Make a plan and commit to it. Watch how intentional time management creates space for purpose to thrive.

Day 27 — Bouncing back from failure

Pain often does what comfort never will. It propels you forward. Not just pain from others, but the pain we cause ourselves. The bad choices, the moments we wish we could undo, the times we failed. Failure doesn't disqualify you. God restores.

David, Moses, Peter, the prodigal son, all of them had failures, and all of them were redeemed. The same God who restored them is the same God who is still writing your story.

Here is where endurance comes in. Breakthrough doesn't come without resistance. Some seasons feel like one challenge after another. You wonder how much more can I take? Here's what you need to know, challenges are the training ground for perseverance.

> "Fear not; you will no longer live in shame. Don't be afraid; there is no more disgrace for you. You will no longer remember the shame of your youth and the sorrows of widowhood."
> Isaiah 54:4

Romans 5:3-4 tells us that suffering produces endurance, endurance builds character, and character strengthens hope. This means that what you are going through is not wasted. It's preparing you. Instead of praying for challenges to end quickly, pray for the strength to endure them well. Be transparent about your journey. Own your failures, but don't let them define you. Address your problems instead of avoiding them.

If you've already fallen, made mistakes, lost time, or feel like you've failed, know that failure is not the end. It's a lesson. Every setback is an opportunity to learn, grow, and refine your approach. Instead of letting failure define you, let it teach you. Ask yourself What did this experience reveal about me? About God? The key to bouncing back is not just getting up, it's getting up wiser.

You are not your mistakes. You are not your past. You are still on track for what God has for you. Keep pressing forward, take the lessons with you, and trust that even in failure God is still working all things together for your good. When you finally step into the fullness of who God created you to be, you'll look back and realize even the pain had a purpose.

JOURNAL PROMPT

What current challenge is testing your endurance? How can you shift your mindset from seeing it as an obstacle to viewing it as preparation for what's next?

_____
_____
_____
_____
_____
_____
_____
_____
_____
_____
_____
_____

Action tip

Identify one failure or setback that has made you feel stuck. Write down three lessons you can take from it and one action you can take to move forward with wisdom. Failure isn't final—it's fuel. Use it to propel you forward.

Day 28 — Your gift is an Assignment

You ever notice how some things just come naturally to you? The way you create, the way you lead, the way you problem solve? How others struggle with something that for you feels effortless? That's not by accident. That's your gift.

Gifts are superpowers from God. They are the things you were designed to do with ease. The abilities woven into you before you even knew their purpose. God gave them to you because He intends to use them through you. Nothing you've learned, endured, or witnessed was a coincidence. Every skill, every lesson, every hardship was all shaping you for a greater assignment. Because your gift is not just about you, it's about what God wants to do through you.

> "God has given each of you a gift from his great variety of spiritual gifts. Use them well to serve one another." – 1 Peter 4:10

This is where purpose comes into play. When you become aware of your gifts you become strategic with your time, your relationships, and your opportunities. You stop wasting energy on things that don't align with your calling. Instead, you start stewarding your gifts with focus because gifts are meant to be given.

We don't hoard them. We share them. We get to be the hands and feet of Jesus on this earth, using what we've been given to serve, uplift, and transform the lives of others.

Your gift is not small. It is not insignificant. It is your assignment. Learn it. Develop it. Activate it. Because when you do, God will move through you in ways that not only change your life but impact everyone connected to you. Step into it. Someone is waiting on what God placed inside of you.

JOURNAL PROMPT

What are the gifts and natural abilities God has placed inside of you? How can you be more intentional in using them to serve others?

_____
_____
_____
_____
_____
_____
_____
_____
_____
_____
_____
_____

Action tip

This week, identify one way you can actively use your gift to impact someone else. Whether it's mentoring, encouraging, creating, teaching, or leading—put your gift into action and watch God move.

Day 29 — Obedience: The Doorway to Purpose

One thing you quickly learn in walking with God is that He will ask you to do things that do not make sense. Things that contradict your logic, challenge your comfort, and stretch your faith in ways you never imagined. Obedience isn't always easy.

Naturally, we want to follow our own desires. We want to take the safest route, the one that makes sense in our minds. But God's instructions often go against our plans. They require us to surrender control and move before we see the full picture. Honesrly that is terrifying.

Obedience is God's love language."If you love me, obey my commandments." – John 14:15 (NLT). Obedience isn't just about following rules. It's about trust. It's about believing that even when we don't understand, God's way is always better. One day you're comfortable in your routine and the next, He's asking you to leave, shift, or start something new. Will you hesitate or will you trust that His instructions are leading you somewhere greater?

> If you are willing and obedient, You shall eat the good of the land. Isaiah 1:19

The beauty of obedience is that it you begin to realize that your success isn't in your hands. It's in God's. He has already mapped out the outcome. All He's asking for is your willingness to take the next step. Growth happens in obedience. Maturity comes from daily decisions to follow His lead, one step at a time.

Today, ask yourself what is God calling you to do that you've been afraid to step into? What if, instead of resisting, you decided to trust? On the other side of your obedience is the purpose, fulfillment, and breakthrough you've been waiting for.

JOURNAL PROMPT

Where is God calling you to be obedient right now? What fears or hesitations have been keeping you from taking the next step?

_____
_____
_____
_____
_____
_____
_____
_____
_____
_____
_____
_____
_____

Action tip

Identify one act of obedience you've been delaying—whether it's making a change, starting something new, or letting go of something that no longer serves you. Commit to taking one step forward this week, trusting that God's plan is leading you exactly where you need to be.

Day 30 — Faith Living

You are at a point where you realize that God is speaking clearly. Maybe it's through a conversation, a song, or even in the quiet moments of your day. The promises He's made for your life begin to take root in your spirit, and you feel the weight of them waiting to unfold. But the truth is those promises don't move without faith. Without faith, those promises sit idle waiting to get in gear.

Faith is what moves God. It's not your performance, your hustle, or even your tears. It's your belief in what He said even when everything around you seems to contradict it. Day in and day out, we're tempted to focus on the chaos of life, the struggles, and setbacks, but faith requires us to look beyond what we see in the natural and trust that God's word carries more weight than any circumstance we face.

> So the promise is received by faith. It is given as a free gift. And we are all certain to receive it. Romans 4:16a

Faith is a weapon, a shield in God's armor. How are we able to fight if we are not protected by the shield that blocks the arrows of doubt, fear, and attacks that Satan fires at us. Think about Joseph. God gave him a dream, but his journey looked nothing like the fulfillment of that promise. Betrayed, sold into slavery, falsely accused, and imprisoned everything around him said, "Give up." Joseph's faith never wavered. He believed in the promise God gave him, and because of his faith, Joseph eventually saw his dream fulfilled.

Here's what we need to hold onto: God's plans for us don't change because of our struggles. If anything, those struggles are shaping us for the promise. Faith alone makes us right in the eyes of God. If you are struggling and need help fueling your faith, David helps us in 1 Chronicles 16. Remember God's covenant and promises made and remember how He's shown up before. If He did it then, He'll do it again. When we persevere in faith, we open the door for God's favor to work in ways we could never imagine.

JOURNAL PROMPT

Write about a promise or dream God has placed on your heart. How does it feel to hold onto that promise in the midst of challenges?

Reflect on a past moment when God showed up for you in a powerful way. How can remembering that moment fuel your faith for what you're waiting on now?

_____
_____
_____
_____
_____
_____
_____
_____
_____
_____
_____
_____

Action tip

Take some time to create a "Faith Fuel List." Write down at least three times in your life when God came through for you in ways you didn't expect. Reflect on these moments daily for the next week, especially when doubt creeps in. If you're facing a specific challenge, find a scripture that speaks to that situation. Write it down and carry it with you as a reminder of God's faithfulness.

Day 31 — Love Like Christ

There is no way to carry out God's heart and His plans without first being a lover of people. We were created to love. Not just in words but in action. Love is not optional. It is our calling. At the core of who God is, He is love and the only way to truly reflect Him in the world is to give that love freely.

Loving people isn't always easy. People will disappoint you. They will misunderstand you. They will sometimes take more than they give but loving as Christ loves means choosing to love anyway.

Love is not a feeling. It's a decision. A decision to be patient when it's easier to react. A decision to show grace when offense tries to creep in. A decision to uplift, inspire, and strengthen those around you even when it's inconvenient.

> "Your love for one another will prove to the world that you are my disciples." – John 13:35

God designed us for relationship. We were never meant to do life alone. Love is what holds us together. It creates unity, builds bridges, and creates a community where people feel valued, accepted, and at peace. This is why you can't fulfill your purpose in isolation. Your purpose is not about you. It's about who you are called to impact. When you walk in love, you create safe spaces where healing happens, where burdens are lifted, and where people experience the heart of God through you.

Position yourself to love well. Love when it's easy. Love when it's hard. Love when you don't feel like it. Love when it costs you something. Because in the end, the greatest testimony you can carry is how well you loved.

JOURNAL PROMPT

How have you been showing love to those around you? Are there any areas where you need to extend more grace, patience, or understanding?

Action tip

Identify one person in your life who may need an extra measure of love and encouragement. Reach out to them today—whether through a message, a prayer, or an act of kindness. Be intentional about reflecting God's love in a tangible way.

Day 32 — Your Body Is Sacred

At the start of anything new, we're bombarded with trends. New diets, gym memberships, body transformations. The pressure to get toned, lose weight, or reshape ourselves to fit society's image of beauty is overwhelming. Social media showcases unrealistic standards, and before we know it, we start measuring ourselves against filters and facades. But have you ever stopped to ask What does God say?

His standard is different. His standard isn't about chasing trends, keeping up with aesthetics, or altering yourself to fit someone else's definition of worthy. His standard is honor. Honoring Him with how you care for yourself. Your body is a temple of the Holy Spirit. That means how you treat it, what you consume, the stress you allow, the environments you enter, the weight you carry all matter. We often focus on avoiding the obvious like certain foods, certain habits, certain sins but what about the hidden things? The stress that wears you down? The spaces you enter that leave you spiritually drained? You are not effective for God's work when you are running on empty.

> "Don't you realize that your body is the temple of the Holy Spirit, who lives in you and was given to you by God? You do not belong to yourself, for God bought you with a high price. So you must honor God with your body." – 1 Corinthians 6:19-20

God designed you to rule, reign, and have dominion. But to do that you need rest, nourishment, self-care, and stamina. You need peace. You need clarity. You can't operate in those things if your body, mind, and spirit are constantly depleted. Shift your perspective. Caring for yourself isn't vanity, it's worship.

It's a way to show gratitude for the life you've been given, for. It's a declaration that you are worthy of care, because the Spirit of God dwells within you. Every decision you make concerning your body reflects your love for Him. Let Him guide what to consume, where to go, what to take on. Receive His rest, wisdom, and His strength, and remember you are a temple. Make it a place where God's Spirit thrives.

JOURNAL PROMPT

In what ways have I neglected caring for my body, mind, or spirit? What steps can I take to honor God with my self-care and wellness?

_____
_____
_____
_____
_____
_____
_____
_____
_____
_____
_____
_____

Action tip

Choose one intentional way to honor God with your body this week—whether it's prioritizing rest, setting a boundary, eating nourishing food, moving your body, or reducing stress. Write it down and commit to it. Let this be your act of worship.

Day 33 — You Are Worth the Investment

We invest in so many things like clothes, vacations, dining out, and entertainment. We swipe our cards without hesitation, spending on everything except the one thing that truly matters: ourselves.

To state the obvious, your growth, healing, and your becoming is worth far more than anything money can buy. Seek counseling, mentorship, or accountability partners to support you

Therapy, coaching, learning a new skill, starting that business, going back to school, whatever it takes to evolve into the woman God created you to be, do it. The money, the time, the energy is not a loss. It's a seed. A seed that will grow, expand, and multiply in ways you can't even imagine.

You are more important than temporary pleasures that leave you empty. The price you pay to become your truest, most God-aligned self is worth it.

Invest in you. Invest in growth. Invest in unlearning what's held you back. Invest in becoming the woman God intended you to be.

> "The Lord will work out his plans for my life—for your faithful love, O Lord, endures forever. Don't abandon me, for you made me." – Psalm 138:8

Don't wait until you feel ready. Readiness is a myth. The fear won't disappear overnight, and comfort won't create change. Step out now. Do something today that your future self and your legacy will thank you for.

This season of becoming won't always feel like this. God is perfecting everything that concerns you. When you look back, you'll see that every sacrifice, every risk, every investment was building the life you were always meant to live.

JOURNAL PROMPT

Where have you been hesitant to invest in yourself—whether financially, emotionally, or spiritually? What's one step you can take today toward your growth and becoming?

_____
_____
_____
_____
_____
_____
_____
_____
_____
_____
_____
_____
_____

Action tip

This week, make one intentional investment in yourself. It could be signing up for a course, scheduling a coaching session, reading a book for growth, or setting aside time for deep reflection and prayer. Whatever it is, commit to it—because your future is worth the investment.

Day 34 — Goals That Align

You weren't created just to cruise through life. You were designed to build, create, and bring forth the vision God has placed inside of you. When God said, "Be fruitful and multiply," He wasn't just talking about having children. He was calling you to produce, to expand, to take what He's given you and grow it into something greater.

Purpose requires direction and direction comes from setting clear, intentional goals while consistently revisiting them to make sure you're staying on course.

> "Look straight ahead, and fix your eyes on what lies before you. Mark out a straight path for your feet; stay on the safe path." – Proverbs 4:25-26

It's not enough to just set goals. You have to check in on your progress. Are you moving forward, or have you stalled? Are your daily actions aligning with your vision, or have you gotten distraction? Is your focus still on God's plan, or have you started pursuing things that only look good but aren't truly aligned?

Life has a way of pulling you in a hundred different directions, and if you're not careful, you can find yourself busy but not productive, moving, but not making progress.

Revisiting your goals keeps you rooted in purpose. You also show God that He can trust you to steward the vision well. Take inventory. Are you still on track with the vision He gave you? Are your goals pushing you toward purpose, or have distractions slowed you down?

Revisit your purpose often. Evaluate where you are and what adjustments need to be made. Sometimes, the vision will evolve. Sometimes, God will refine it. But you'll only know if you take time to reflect and realign.

JOURNAL PROMPT

What goals have you set for yourself this year? Are you actively working toward them, or have distractions pulled you off course? What steps can you take this week to realign?

_____
_____
_____
_____
_____
_____
_____
_____
_____
_____
_____
_____

Action tip

Take 30 minutes this week to review your vision and goals. Write down what progress you've made, what adjustments need to be made, and set a plan for your next steps.

Day 35

Your Testimony is Someone's Breakthrough

There is power in your story. Not the polished version, not the version that skips over the struggles, but the real, raw, unfiltered truth of what you've been through and how God brought you out. Your testimony is evidence that God is real.

Someone needs to hear it. There are people going through what you've already survived. They are wondering if God still moves, still heals, still restores. Your testimony is living proof that He does.

It reminds the weary that miracles still happen. It strengthens the faith of those who feel like giving up. It gives hope to those who think they're too far gone.

When you open your mouth to testify, you are giving an invitation for others to experience the same God who transformed your life.

> "Come and listen, all you who fear God, and I will tell you what he did for me." – Psalm 66:16

God wants witnesses. Not just people who read about Him, but people who have experienced Him. People who have seen Him make a way, heal their bodies, restore their minds, provide when there was nothing left, bring peace in the middle of chaos. People who won't keep silent about what they've seen and heard.

What is your testimony? What prayers has God answered? What doors has He opened? What storms has He brought you through? Take a moment and reflect. Not just on what God has done for you, but on the power of sharing it. Because when you share your testimony, you're not just telling your story, you're building someone else's faith. You're letting someone else know, "If He did it for me, He can do it for you too." That's the kind of impact that changes lives.

JOURNAL PROMPT

What is one testimony in your life that could encourage someone else? How can you share it in a way that builds faith and points back to God's power?

_____
_____
_____
_____
_____
_____
_____
_____
_____
_____
_____
_____

Action tip

Find one person this week—a friend, family member, or even a social media post—to share your testimony with. Big or small, your story carries power. Be bold in telling what God has done. Someone is waiting to hear it.

Day 36

Start where you are

You may not have the full picture yet. You may feel like you're in transition, unsure of what's next, standing at the edge of something new but unable to see the full picture ahead. All of that is okay. Start where you are.

We often think that purpose has to be fully revealed before we can move but that's not how God works. Before you know the details of your unique calling, there's a universal one.

Love God. Love people. Serve those in need. Share your testimony. That alone is enough to begin. Your first step is obedience. God magnifies your efforts when you trust Him enough to start, even when you don't have all the answers.

> "Do not despise these small beginnings, for the Lord rejoices to see the work begin." – Zechariah 4:10

Maybe you've been feeling restless. That stirring inside? It's not random. it's confirmation that you've been idle too long. God is calling you to move with urgency. Not because you need to have everything figured out, but because He will guide your steps as you walk. Stop waiting for clarity before you take action. Clarity comes in motion.

Here's the beauty of small beginnings. They are tests. God watches what you do with what's in your hands right now before He releases more into your life. When He sees that you are faithful with little, He knows He can trust you with much. (Luke 16:10) The blessings you're praying for are often tied to your willingness to move, even when it feels insignificant. The opportunities and the increase all starts when you show up, stay consistent, and trust that God rewards obedience.

Don't despise the small things. God sees them, He honors them, and He multiplies them. Your next level is on the other side of your first step. It's time. Take the first step and watch what happens next.

JOURNAL PROMPT

Where have you been waiting for clarity before taking action? What is one step you can take today, trusting that God will reveal more as you move?

_____
_____
_____
_____
_____
_____
_____
_____
_____
_____
_____
_____

Action tip

Identify one small action you can take this week toward living in purpose—whether it's serving someone, sharing your story, or stepping out in faith in a new way. Write it down, commit to it, and do it. Watch how God meets you in your movement.

Day 37
The Power of Balance: Avoiding Burnout

Balancing career, home, responsibilities, and commitments are no small task. Some days it feels like you're juggling a thousand things at once, trying to be everything for everyone. If you are being honest, you're exhausted. You're not alone.

Burnout is real and it doesn't just happen all at once. It creeps in slowly. Like a phone overloaded with too many apps running at the same time, you start slowing down. Freezing. Crashing, and just like a phone needs a reset to function properly, so do you.

> "Then Jesus said, 'Come to me, all of you who are weary and carry heavy burdens, and I will give you rest.'" – Matthew 11:28

Balance is not about doing everything perfectly. It's about finding rhythm. knowing when to push forward and when to pause.
Balance looks like this:
• Learning to be content where you are, while still striving for where you're going.
• Taking intentional breaks before burnout forces you to stop.
• Giving yourself permission to rest, guilt-free, because your well-being matters.
• Prioritizing self-care, personal relationships, and your spiritual journey—not just your to-do list.

Without balance stress builds, anxiety rises, and joy disappears, but when you intentionally make space for both ambition and rest, you find peace. You gain clarity. You wake up feeling present instead of drained, fulfilled instead of frustrated. You deserve to live a life that doesn't just look good, but feels good.

Today, let's reset. Step away when needed. Rest before you're forced to. Make space for what gives you joy. Success isn't just about how much you accomplish. It's about how well you live while accomplishing it.

JOURNAL PROMPT

Where in your life have you been overextending yourself? What small changes can you make to create a healthier balance between work, relationships, and self-care?

_____
_____
_____
_____
_____
_____
_____
_____
_____
_____
_____
_____

Action tip

This week, schedule intentional rest. Whether it's a quiet moment in the morning, an afternoon break, or an evening off from responsibilities—prioritize yourself. Rest is not a reward; it's a necessity. Give yourself permission to reset.

Day 38

Setting Boundaries

Boundaries are not walls. They are the limits that protect your peace, energy, and purpose. For too long, we've been taught that saying "yes" to everything makes us good, selfless, or valuable but the truth is, a life without boundaries leads to exhaustion, resentment, and imbalance.

When you don't set limits, people will take as much as you allow. Boundaries are necessary. They are a reflection of self-respect, clarity, and wisdom.

> "Guard your heart above all else, for it determines the course of your life." – Proverbs 4:23

Boundaries in relationships protect your heart from unhealthy connections. Boundaries in work prevent burnout and ensure you don't sacrifice yourself for success. Boundaries with your time allow you to prioritize what truly matters. Boundaries with yourself keep you disciplined and committed to your growth.

Setting boundaries is just the beginning. You must also uphold them. People will test your boundaries. Situations will challenge them, but you must stand firm.

When you uphold your boundaries, here's what happens
- You experience peace because your energy is protected.
- You become more confident in making decisions without guilt.
- You attract healthier relationships that honor and respect your limits.
- You grow spiritually and emotionally because you're no longer drained by what isn't serving you.

The more you reinforce your boundaries, the stronger you become. The stronger you become, the more space you create for God's best in your life. Give yourself permission to set boundaries without apology. Don't feel guilty, or second guess. When you honor your boundaries, you honor yourself, and the purpose God has placed within you.

JOURNAL PROMPT

Where in your life have you allowed boundaries to be crossed? How can you reinforce them in a way that protects your peace and purpose?

_____
_____
_____
_____
_____
_____
_____
_____
_____
_____
_____
_____

Action tip

This week, identify one boundary you need to strengthen. Write it down, communicate it clearly, and uphold it without guilt. Whether it's saying "no" to something that drains you or prioritizing time for yourself, stand firm and protect what matters.

Day 39 — Stay the Course

Desire gets you started, but determination and commitment are what carry you through. It's one thing to dream about where you want to be. It's another to stay the course when the journey gets hard. Being honest, starting is easy. Finishing is where the battle is.

The space between who you are now and who you're becoming is filled with challenges, and moments that make you want to quit. The process of growth is beautiful but exhausting, transformative but tiring. Some days, you're motivated. Other days, you feel like you're stuck in an emotional rollercoaster of frustration, and uncertainty, but don't stop now.

> Being confident of this, that he who began a good work in you will carry it on to completion until the day of Christ Jesus - Philippians 1:6

God is preparing you for what He has prepared for you. Every challenge is shaping you. Every delay is refining you. Every lesson is equipping you. This is not the time to shrink back or sell yourself short.

Life will throw obstacles your way. People will doubt you. Fear will try to paralyze you. Circumstances will make you question if you even heard God correctly, but the ones who experience God's richest blessings are the ones who stay the course.

You are not behind. You are not failing. You are becoming. Stay faithful. Stay committed. Stay the course. The joy on the other side is worth every sacrifice. You got this.

JOURNAL PROMPT

Where in your life have you been tempted to give up?
What would it look like to stay the course despite the challenges?

_____
_____
_____
_____
_____
_____
_____
_____
_____
_____
_____
_____
_____

Action tip

Identify one failure or setback that has made you feel stuck. Write down three lessons you can take from it and one action you can take to move forward with wisdom. Failure isn't final—it's fuel. Use it to propel you forward.

Day 40 — Celebrate the Journey

Stepping into your purpose isn't just about knowing what you're called to do. It's about walking in it with confidence, endurance, and gratitude. Wholeness isn't a destination, it's a journey.

You are constantly evolving, growing, and maturing in Christ. Every challenge you overcome, every lesson you learn, is shaping you into the woman God designed you to be. Remember to take time to celebrate how far you've come.

Too often, we get so focused on the next goal, the next breakthrough that we don't pause to acknowledge the progress we've already made. Celebrating your growth isn't prideful but necessary.

It reminds you that you're not where you used to be. It builds momentum, motivating you to keep going. It strengthens your faith.

> "Do not despise these small beginnings, for the Lord rejoices to see the work begin."
> – Zechariah 4:10

If no one else claps for you, clap for yourself. There will be seasons where your victories are unseen, where the progress you make isn't acknowledged by others. That doesn't mean it's not worth celebrating. Your obedience, faithfulness, perseverance all matters.

As you celebrate, stay grounded in humility and gratitude. Never forget who you are and what God has done for you. Your success isn't just about you. It's about the impact, the influence, and the transformation God wants to create through you. Pause. Reflect. Celebrate. Then, with humility and boldness, keep going. Because the journey doesn't end here. This is just the beginning.

JOURNAL PROMPT

What personal milestones have you overlooked or downplayed? How can you intentionally celebrate your growth and use it as motivation to keep moving forward?

_____
_____
_____
_____
_____
_____
_____
_____
_____
_____

Action tip

Take a moment to write down five victories from your journey—big or small. Then, thank God for each one. Whether it's a step in faith, a challenge you overcame, or a lesson you learned, celebrate what He's already done as you continue moving toward what's next.

My professional journey began in healthcare, where I worked as a Physical Therapist Assistant for over a decade. During this time, I worked in various settings, including roles as Director and Assistant Director of Rehabilitation, and took pride in mentoring students in clinical settings. My work was rooted in helping others heal physically, but it quickly became evident that I had a deeper calling. I found myself supporting not just the physical, but also the mental and emotional well-being of my clients. I've always been drawn to helping people rebuild their lives, discover their strengths, and find purpose beyond their circumstances.

Today, I bring that same dedication and empathy into the work I do with my clients. My skills are a unique blend of:
• Purpose Development: Guiding women to uncover hidden gifts, heal from their past, and create lives of impact and fulfillment.
• Personal Breakthroughs: Leveraging my expertise in overcoming challenges to help clients break free from limiting beliefs, push beyond their perceived limits, and confidently embrace their next steps.
• Faith-Based Empowerment: Drawing from my undeniable faith, I provide spiritual encouragement and practical tools to help my audience align with their God-given purpose.

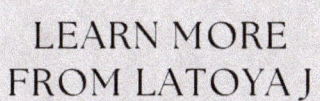

LEARN MORE
FROM LATOYA J

www.latoyaj.com

@LATOYA JACKSON
@IAM_LATOYAJ
@IAM_LATOYAJ
@IAM_LATOYAJ
COACHLATOYAJ@GMAIL.COM

www.ingramcontent.com/pod-product-compliance
Lightning Source LLC
Chambersburg PA
CBHW051214290426
44109CB00021B/2449